N   1998.

To the girls & boys in

with love,

Pat.

x

MW01710666

LOOKING AT THE XHOSA

Photographs and Text by
Roger and Pat de la Harpe

STRUIK

The sun is warm and the familiar smell of the goats and grass is comforting as Malume and his grandfather walk across the Eastern Cape veld. The old man *(madala)* is hunched over and leans on his stick to help him along the narrow paths. It seems to Malume, however, that he walks a little taller and that his tired eyes sparkle as he speaks about how the Xhosa had never been conquered by the powerful Zulu Chief Shaka, and how they had fiercely defended their land when the early White settlers had moved up from the Cape Colony.

Suddenly tired of hearing about the past, the young boy is pleased when his village *(umuzi)* comes into view. A Xhosa home is a round hut with a thatched roof and sometimes it has designs painted on the outside. Several families build their huts in a group and the doors all face the cattle pen which is close by. When a new hut is built, everybody in the community helps. First the men make a framework of branches and then the women plaster the walls with mud and thatch the roof.

Malume catches sight of his sister, Nomsisi, helping their mother sort sugar beans for the evening meal. These, along with maize and sour milk, are the main foods eaten by the Xhosa people. They eat the maize either as kernels or, after it has been finely ground, as a stiff porridge. They also serve pumpkin and wild spinach but only eat meat on special occasions. A thick beer is regularly made from maize and it is the custom for those in a group to drink the beer from the same container as it is passed around.

The children are expected to help around the home but, in spite of their chores, they still find time to play in the fields and streams near their village. From an early age the girls help their mothers with the cooking, collecting firewood and water *(amanzi)* and looking after their younger brothers and sisters. The boys tend their father's cattle and goats and make sure that the animals are home for milking in the evening. Around the fire at meal times the children learn about Xhosa customs and traditions from their parents and elders.

Malume and Nomsisi's mother prepares to go to the trading store to buy beads and buttons to decorate her new skirt. As a married woman her skirts are ankle-length and she wears a turban elaborately wrapped around her head (above). Young girls wear shorter skirts and a beaded headband or a flat turban. The traditional man's headdress is also a turban (right) and both men and women wear togas around their shoulders that are usually white or dyed red with ochre. The Xhosa love beadwork and the men especially look very colourful at ceremonies and other social gatherings.

After returning from the trading store their mother and her friends get together to smoke their pipes and to chat. Pipes are passed around among the people in a group and anybody who has tobacco shares it with the others. The stem of the pipe is sometimes covered with beads and a woman's pipe has a longer stem than a man's. Both men and women carry tobacco pouches that are made from either cloth or animal skin and are decorated with beads, buttons and braid.

Malume helps his older brother fix the stone wall of the cattle pen. Cattle and goats are the wealth of a Xhosa family and looking after them is the job of the father and his sons. The men build the pen in a circle, using either branches or stones. It is close to the huts so that the families can hear any unusual sounds coming from the pen during the night. The cattle pen is a place where the cows are milked, but it is also a sacred place where the men pray to their ancestral spirits, whom they believe influence their lives.

Malume looks forward to taking part in these ceremonies in the cattle pen, but he will have to wait until he is about 17 years of age or older. A Xhosa boy is not considered a man until he has gone through an initiation ritual that takes about three months. During this time the boys are taught about different traditions and how to behave as men. At the end of the three months they go back to their villages and are then expected to behave in a responsible way and to begin thinking of getting married within the next few years.

Three years have passed since their brother's initiation and he is soon to marry. A Xhosa man may have more than one wife, but these days it does not happen often as marriage is expensive. He pays for his bride in cattle and his future father-in-law usually asks for 11 animals as payment *(lobola)* for his daughter. The first wife is the most important and she is known as the 'great wife' while the second wife is known as the 'little wife'. They share the duties and chores around the home and in the fields.

Like their friends, Malume and Nomsisi love to sing and dance, and many of their dances tell tales of Xhosa history. The children dance on their own or in a group whenever they can and, of course, at ceremonies. They clap, stamp their feet and blow whistles during the dancing (right). Stick fighting (above) is a great sport among the boys and they spend hours competing against each other, especially over the weekends. Even young boys, like Malume, have their own sticks.

At night the family keeps the door and windows of their hut closed so that no evil spirits can come in while they are sleeping. The Xhosa people believe that certain birds and animals have magical powers and that the lightning bird *(impundulu)*, the water snake *(ichanti)* and the baboon *(imfene)* are all used by witches to bring bad luck. A diviner uses special medicines to protect people from evil, and also talks to the ancestral spirits via a small beaded calabash (above). A sick person visits a traditional healer who gives him mixtures of bark, roots and herbs to help him feel better.

A few Xhosa words Malume and Nomsisi think you should know:

Hello	*Molo*
Please	*Nceda*
Thank you	*Nkozi*
Go	*Hamba*
Water	*Amanzi*
Bride price	*Lobola*
Old man	*Madala*
Lightning bird	*Impundulu*
Water snake	*Ichanti*
Baboon	*Imfene*
Village	*Umuzi*

Acknowledgement
The authors would like to thank the staff of Lesedi Cultural Village in Johannesburg for their assistance.

Struik Publishers (Pty) Ltd
(a member of The Struik Publishing Group (Pty) Ltd)
Cornelis Struik House
80 McKenzie Street
Cape Town 8001

Reg. No.: 54/00965/07

First published in 1998

Editor: Glynne Newlands
Concept design: Laurence Lemmon-Warde
Designer: Dominic Robson
Cover design: Dominic Robson

Reproduction: Unifoto (Pty) Ltd
Printing and binding:
National Book Printers, Drukkery Street, Goodwood, Western Cape

ISBN 1 86872 127 2